# DERBY TRAMWAYS

## Colin Barker

*Series editor Robert J. Harley*

**MP** Middleton Press

*Cover picture: A rebuilt car from the original delivery of 1904 waits at the stop on the London Road leg of The Spot on its way to Midland Station. The motorman looks for the all clear to move off whilst the lower deck passengers rest on the peripheral seating. (Author's collection)*

*Cover colours: The colours used on the cover are similar to the Derby Corparation Tramways green and cream livery.*

**Published to mark the electric tramway centenary in 2004.**

*First Published October 2003*

*ISBN  1 904474  17 9*

*© Middleton Press, 2003*

*Design  David Pede*

*Published by*
> *Middleton Press*
> *Easebourne Lane*
> *Midhurst, West Sussex*
> *GU29 9AZ*

*Tel: 01730 813169*
*Fax: 01730 812601*
*Email: info@middletonpress.co.uk*
*www.middletonpress.co.uk*

*Printed & bound by Biddles Ltd, Kings Lynn*

# CONTENTS

# INTRODUCTION AND ACKNOWLEDGEMENTS

Following the publication of my book *Derby Trolleybuses*, the Editor asked me to consider a similar publication on Derby Tramways.

Earlier publications on Derby's public transport have included a comprehensive route history (Barry Edwards and John Simpson, Omnibus Society 1983) and two detailed books by Barry Edwards *Derby Transport 1840-1945* (Clay Kingsley Press 1986) and *The Story of Transport in Derby* (Breedon Books 1993). A publication, largely of pictorial content, by Alan Doig and Maxwell Craven *Derby Trams and Buses Volume 1* (Trent Valley Publications) also appeared in 1986. All of these publications had photographic coverage of the tram era.

There were not many transport enthusiasts with cameras in the early 1900s and it was only in the late 1920s and early 1930s that a few began to record the system for future generations. To them we are indebted. The sources were therefore mainly restricted to the material of professional photographers, particularly W.W. Winter, official views, equipment manufacturers and commercial postcards.

Whilst the horse tram had provided basic public transport to some areas of the town, the advent of electric trams over a much wider area gave the general population a cheap, reliable and faster means of going about their everyday business. The only means of transport before the introduction of electric trams was to cycle, be drawn by a horse or, if you were very well off, have the benefit of one of the early unreliable motorcars. The electric tramway therefore had a major impact on the town's development.

The photographic sequence follows the various routes from the two central termini, namely the Market Place and Victoria Street. The views originate from a variety of sources; where the photographer or organisation is known, due credit has been given. Inevitably some views give no indication as to their originators. Their work has been chosen with good intent in order to enhance this publication for a wider audience.

Thanks go to Barry Edwards and Philip Thomas for their constructive comments in reading through the first draft and to John Gillham for the use of his comprehensive route map. Barry Edwards also provided the copy tickets. Thanks also to Rosemary Thacker and Glynn Wilton at the Crich Tramway Museum, Mark Higgingson at the Derby Industrial Museum and Vivien Rudd at Derby Museum for providing material from within their archives. Finally, I would like to thank my editor Robert Harley for encouraging me to take on this venture and to my wife, Maureen, for her support and word processing skills.

In July 2004 it will be 100 years since the opening of the electric tramway in Derby; it is perhaps too much to imagine the return of railed electric public transport to Derby's city centre streets.

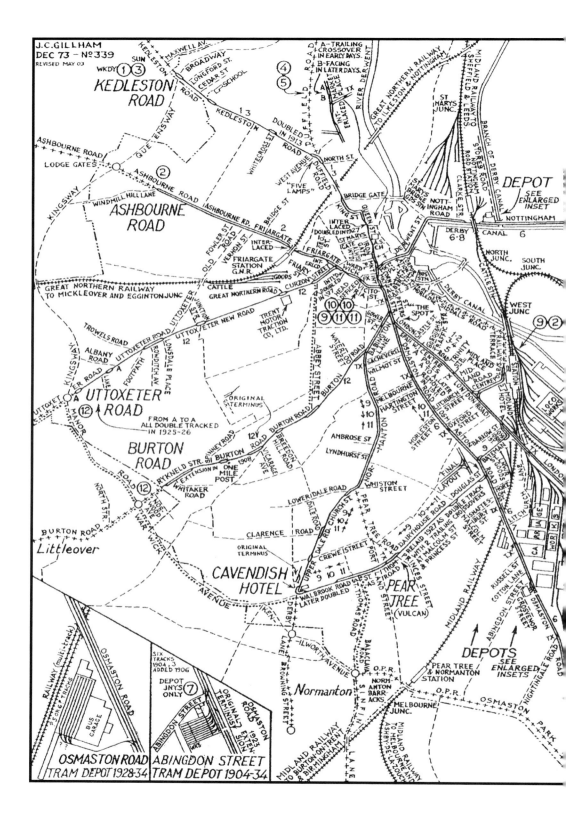

from Osmaston Road to The Vulcan (destination Pear Tree) via Douglas Street and Dairyhouse Road.

Track and overhead were opened down the short length of the Cornmarket and into the Market Place on 24th February 1905 and the Alvaston departures transferred from Victoria Street.

On 31st July 1905 the Kedleston Road horse bus route was converted and extended near to what is now the junction with Broadway.

The next major development was the linking of the Cavendish and The Vulcan on 5th September 1905 via Walbrook Road and St Thomas Road. This provided circular routes from town in both directions out via either Normanton Road or Osmaston Road. There was also a route to the Midland Station via Normanton Road and the Cavendish.

Next to be converted were Ashbourne Road and Uttoxeter Road on 28th November 1907 with the former terminating at Windmill Hill Lane and the latter being extended from the Rowditch horse bus terminus to near the site of the current Manor Road/Kingsway junction.

1908 saw the last pre-war conversions comprising Nottingham Road on 8th February 1908 and the extension of the Burton Road route to a terminus adjacent to Farley Road on 30th July 1908. Various coloured lights indicated routes until the introduction of route number indicator boxes in 1917/18.

The final extension came after the First World War and opened on 4th August 1923 when the Osmaston Road route was extended from Abingdon Street to a point adjacent to Osmaston Park Road.

By the end of the 1920s there was a need for capital expenditure to refurbish deteriorating vehicles and track, bearing in mind that in common with most tramway systems there had been a general lack of maintenance between 1914-18 and immediately afterwards. Increased motor traffic also caused difficulties with the inevitable conflict with railed vehicles. The Corporation however owned the electricity generating equipment and the underground distribution cables still had many years of life left. These factors, together with the need for route extensions, led to a debate on the use of trolleybuses.

In 1930 a special committee was set up and after exhaustive deliberations the replacement of the trams with trolleybuses was recommended. The building of the new Exeter Bridge over the River Derwent determined the first route to be converted, namely Nottingham Road, especially as there was the depot at Stores Road. Tram access was provided over the new bridge whilst it was under construction, but trams ceased on 14th November 1930 and motorbuses substituted (and extended to Lime Grove) whilst the conversion of the depot for trolleybuses and the extending of the route to The Creamery was completed ready for the opening on 9th January 1932.

The use of trolleybuses was a success and a full conversion programme put in place with trams ceasing on Burton Road/Uttoxeter Road on 9th January 1932, being replaced by motorbuses pending the introduction of trolleybuses on 13th August 1933. The former was extended to Chain Lane, Littleover and the latter to Corden Avenue. London Road followed with a one-day conversion to motorbuses on 23rd July 1932 and the trolleybuses taking over the next day to a terminus along Harvey Road at Wyndham Street.

Trams on Osmaston Road ceased on 12th November 1932 apart from workman and depot workings; trolleybuses took over the next day and the route was extended to Allenton. Trams ceased on Kedleston Road on 12th August 1933 and motorbuses substituted only to be followed by a conversion to trolleybuses on 28th April 1935 with an extension to Allestree Lane End. Ashbourne Road followed with trams finishing on 30th December 1933 and trolleybuses operating to Kingsway the next day.

The final conversion comprised the Normanton Road/Cavendish/Pear Tree routes with the tram services ceasing on 17th March 1934 and trolleybuses taking over the next day. Trams continued on certain workman specials until 30th June 1934 with the official closure of the tramway system taking place on 2nd July.

Thus ended 54 years of railed street public transport in Derby, which had commenced with the horse trams in 1880 and, with the final 30 years electrically powered. Electric traction was to continue for a further 33 years with the advent of the trolleybuses. The trolleybus era is described in companion Middleton Press volume *Derby Trolleybuses*.

# POINTS AND CROSSINGS.

Material.

42. The whole of the points shall be of British manufacture, and ma entirely of the very best manganese steel. The castings produced are to be suitab for hard wear, perfectly sound, and free from sand holes, air pockets, honeycom and other imperfections, and without flaws of any description, and to the enti satisfaction of the Borough Surveyor. No plugging or filling of cavities or blo holes will be permitted, but small defects may be electrically welded, subject the consent of the Inspector.

Tests of Materials.

43. The manganese steel will be subject to forge tests, and excess materi is to be left on a percentage of the castings for this purpose, and broken off the presence of the Inspector. Analysis for manganese and carbon may also l made by an independent chemist, and cost charged to the Contractor, but su charges will be limited to half of one per cent. on the value of the contrac Bending tests may also be made.

Points.

44. The whole of the castings for points (unless otherwise especially ordered whether automatic spring, movable or fixed points, etc., to be of a minimu length of 12 ft., the points for diamond loops being 200 ft. equal radius, and f the lateral loops 150 ft. radius, with ample length of rail section for attac ment to the end of rails, drawing of which with fish-plate, etc., is append hereto, such lengths of rail section to be provided with holes as required f attachment to rails, fish-plates, holding-down girders, etc., in such a manner an of such an approved pattern and design, and to be made in such a way as avoid any cutting of rails, to engage truly up to the ends of rails, leaving th tops perfectly true and in line with the grooves in the casting, and to allow the fish-plates to fit perfectly thereto. The tongues to be 8 ft. long, made manganese steel, and for automatic points to be held in position by good stron springs fitted in boxes by the sides of the points and provided with covers to giv access to the same for renewal and adjustment, and also with suitable provision for drainage. The springs to be adjustable and the tongues to fit all along th bearing surfaces in their castings, and to be machined or grooved accuratel throughout. The movable points to be similar to the above in all respects, wit the exception of the spring, and shall be fitted with suitable mechanism to preven the tongue moving from the position in which it is placed or remaining centra

An extract from the contract for the track.

# HORSE POWER TO ELECTRIC TRACTION

1.      Horse trams provided public transport services in Derby for over 27 years and this wonderful view of St Peter's Street in the early 1880s depicts a hive of activity. Two horse trams, including Car 12 from the oridginal delivery of 1880/81, stand in the passing loop outside St Peter's Church waiting for the third tram to climb towards Babington Lane: note there is no trace horse to help with the climb. The five Midland Railway drays in the foreground, and at least one in the distance, are carrying chests of tea; perhaps by coincidence the shop on the corner of East Street belongs to The Star Tea Company. (Derby Local Studies Library.  Ref.DRBY 001651)

2.      The old and the new seen sometime between 8th September 1904 and 1st June 1907, when horse trams ceased along Ashbourne Road.  Three electric cars await departure from Victoria Street with the upper deck destination of Car 5 in the foreground set for Pear Tree and the front dash display indicating the journey is via Osmaston Road.  Horse tram 22, bound for Ashbourne Road, is an ex-Glasgow car that was one of six purchased in 1902/3.  (J.S.Simnett)

# MARKET PLACE

3.    This 1930s view, taken from the south side of the Market Place looking towards Derwent Street, shows Car 2 on Route 7 to Osmaston Road depot. Although still in original open top condition, the platforms have been modified to give the motorman protection from the elements. The building on the right was originally the Royal Oak public house and now houses the solicitors Flint Bishop & Barnett, although it was used as the Town Clerk's office from 1920. (Author's coll.)

4.    A wonderfully atmospheric view of a car from the 26-29 batch outside the offices of the *Derbyshire Advertiser* newspaper on the south side of the Market Place; next door is Frost's Pork Store.  The destination is Osmaston Road as the motorman helps the family with the pushchair. Judging from the clothing, particularly the gentleman in plus fours, this is a post 1929 view. (Author's coll.)

5. Also seen outside the *Advertiser* offices is one of the two short length cars, either 40 or 41, delivered in 1907 that had a distance of only 12'6" (3810mm) between bulkheads. When the order for seven single deck cars from Milnes Voss was reduced to four it was agreed two short double deckers plus three others (42-44) would be taken in lieu.
(W. Gratwicke via Science Museum. Ref. W6244)

6. One of the four single deck cars, numbered 36-39, purchased from an initial order for seven to negotiate Friargate railway bridge, waits at the Alvaston stand on the western side of the Market Place before departing on a short working to Brighton Road. Car 38 was the subject of a Corgi model. (Author's coll.)

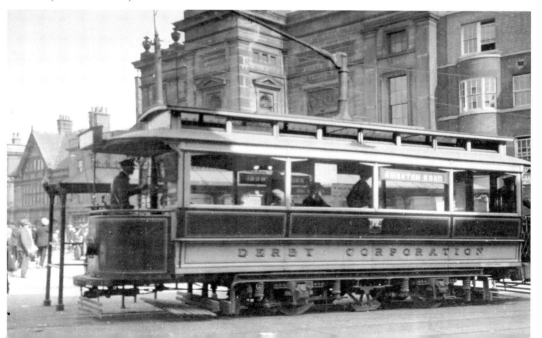

7.    A car from the 45-47 batch leads this pair waiting on the west side of the Market Place. The lattice gate has been closed to prevent passengers entering the front platform that is the motorman's domain for the outward journey. The car to the rear is 50 and the view dates from about 1930. (Author's coll.)

8.    Car 51, a balcony car delivered in June 1920, waits at the Alvaston stand which was erected in 1919. The open tourer on the left would look well at any current vintage car rally. (Author's coll. Commercial postcard)

9.    A quiet Sunday Market Place scene with Car 76 from the last delivery in 1927 waiting to depart for Osmaston Road. The through running to Nottingham Road of this service was discontinued in November 1930 to allow the section between the Market Place and Nottingham Road to be converted for the introduction of the first trolleybuses to The Creamery in January 1932, with motorbuses covering to Lime Grove during the intervening period. In the background, Car 68 enters Irongate past the Barlow Taylor store on the Sunday Route 3 between Alvaston and Kedleston Road. (S.L.Smith)

# IRONGATE/FIVE LAMPS/KEDLESTON ROAD

1.   The cathedral tower of All Saints provides the background for Car 27 in Irongate as it enters double track to drop down into the Market Place and then onwards to the Midland Station.  On the right is an early motor car registered R636, whilst the sun blind of the shop on the corner of Amen Alley in the background protects the goods of the Furniture Market.
(Author's coll. Commercial postcard)

12.    Car 77 en route to Kedleston Road reaches the top of Queen Street and is about to take the sharp left hand bend into Kings Street in about 1930.  The original St Alkmunds Church is in the background and St Michaels is on the right.  The policeman walks purposefully towards the town centre passed a parked Trent charabanc.  (Barry Edwards coll. Commercial postcard)

13.    This view from a postcard produced by Lever Brothers of Derby is interesting in that the postmark is only 17 days after the opening of the Kedleston Road route on 31st July 1905.  Car 1 is seen at the Five Lamps junction of Kedleston Road and Duffield Road.  The tarmac strip along the pavement on the left may be the trench in which the electric supply cables were laid to feed the overhead.  The lamps are to the right of the tram.  (Author's coll. Commercial postcard)

14. A view from the Wheeldon Avenue/Redshaw Street junction with Car 8 passing large Victorian houses many of which were occupied by the senior officers of the Midland Railway. (Author's coll. Commercial postcard)

1904

# DERBY

# Corporation Tramways

---◆---

# TIME TABLE.

## WEEK DAYS.

### Midland Station, Market Place,
### AND
### Kedleston Road Route.

(Red Light).

| FOR MIDLAND STATION. | FOR MARKET PLACE. |
|---|---|
| Cars leave Market Place every 5 minutes from 7.40 a.m. to 10 p.m. then every 10 minutes until 11 p.m. | Cars leave Midland Station every 5 minutes from 7.45 a.m. to 10 p.m. then every 10 minutes until 11 p.m. |

#### SUNDAYS.

| | |
|---|---|
| Cars leave the Market Place every 10 minutes from 6.5 p.m. to 10.5 p.m. | Cars leave Midland Station every 10 minutes from 6.5 p.m. to 10.5 p.m. |

## MID. STATION & MARKET PLACE—contd.

The 10 5 p.m. Car from Market Place runs from Midland Station, via Bateman Street, to Car Depot. *Fare*, 1d. each way.

### STOPPING STATIONS.

Royal Hotel, St. Peter's Street, St. Peter's Church, The Spot, Devonshire Street, Castle Street, Traffic Street, Liversage Street, Royal Infirmary, Canal Street, Regent Street, Park Street, Midland Railway Station.

### Midland Station, Market Place, and Kedleston Road.

| Leave Midland Station. a.m. | Leave Market Place. | Through Cars from Kedleston Road to Midland Station leave the Terminus at 7.30 a.m., and every 10 minutes until 10.50.p.m. |
|---|---|---|
| ,, | 7 20 | |
| ,, | 7 30 | |
| ,, | 7 40 | |
| 7 50 | 7 50 | The 11 p.m and 11.10 p.m. Cars run to the Market Place only, also the 11.20 p.m. Saturdays. |
| and every 10 minutes until | 8 0 | |
| 10 50 p.m. 11 0 pm | | |

*Saturdays only.*
Last Car leaves Station at 11 p.m., Market Place at 11.10 p.m.

Fares, to and from Market Place, 1d.
,, ,, Midland Station, 2d.

### STOPPING STATIONS.

Market Place, All Saints' Church, St. Alkmund's Church, King Street, Lodge Lane, Five Lamps, "Duffield Road," Whitecross Street, Cowley Street, Cedar Terrace, Cedar Street, Terminus.

15.     A balcony car arrives at the terminus of the Kedleston Road route which was at Penny Long Lane; this was roughly where Broadway joins Kedleston Road today.  The tram will travel forward onto the single track before moving back to the stop ready to return to town.  Seats have conveniently been provided for waiting passengers against the background of the property that became the Clovelly Hotel.  (Don Gwinnett coll.  Commercial postcard)

| Ja | **8003** | |
|---|---|---|
| DERBY CORPORATION TRAMWAYS | | |
| Kedleston Road | **1½d** Ked. | Royal Fl.... |
| Belper Road | | M.... 1d Station Midland Road |
| Market Place | This ticket must be punched in the presence of the passenger and is available in section indicated by punch hole. To be shown on demand. | Deadmans Lane |
| Midland Road | | Brighton Road |
| Carr. Wks. Gates | | Alvaston |
| Ashbourne Road | | Victoria Street |
| Uttoxeter Old Road | | Midland Station |
| To Car Depot | | From Car Depot |

# DERWENT STREET/NOTTINGHAM ROAD

16.    This late 1920s view well illustrates the crossroads for the future of trams in Derby.  Horse drawn traffic is still around, but motorised traffic is on the increase, although the lorry still has solid tyres.  On the right the new Exeter Bridge over the River Derwent is under construction which, when completed, will be devoid of tram track thereby leaving the Nottingham Road Depot isolated from the rest of the system and available for fitting out ready for the initial Nottingham Road trolleybus conversion.  Car 45 makes its way across the old river bridge towards the Market Place. (Author's coll.)

17.    At the end of Derwent Street Car 33 crosses the bridge over the Derby Canal before making a sharp right hand turn into Nottingham Road.  It was delivered in 1906 as a covered balcony car but has had motorman protection added.  The scene is post 1917 and is unrecognisable today being roughly where the underpass from Derwent Street passes under the St Alkmunds Way section of the Inner Ring Road.  (Author's coll.)

18.     A car on interlaced track passes under the bridge on Nottingham Road which carries the railway line north to Sheffield, Leeds and Manchester. Nottingham Road station was on the right with the entrance immediately beyond the bridge. The original road level can be clearly seen being lowered part width on the left when the bridge was built. This section was lowered twice to accommodate trams and yet again full road width when trolleybuses were introduced. Note the overhead feeder cables in the foreground and the entrance to the Nottingham Road Depot and permanent way yard on the right. (Courtesy of the *Derby Evening Telegraph*)

19.     Car 46 climbs Cemetery Hill, Nottingham Road, having just left a passing loop to enter the single track to the terminus just beyond the cemetery gates at the top of the hill.
(Author's coll. Commercial postcard)

20.    A busy scene in the Cornmarket between January 1906 and November 1907 depicts Car 33 making its way to the Market Place on the Alvaston route. From the latter date the Alvaston service was linked with Uttoxeter Road and hence routed via Victoria Street. The horse drawn cabs wait for hire on the left whilst the buildings on the right include The Maypole Dairy, Salman and Gluckstein (tobacconist) and the striped gable end of the Old Angel bar. Also note the mobile advertising. (Author's coll. Commercial postcard)

21.    A similar view, but this time in the late 1920s, is of Car 22 rebuilt to fully enclose design from its original open top open platform specification; it will soon make the return journey to Alvaston from the Market Place on Route 4. The Alvaston route returned to the Market Place in 1922 when the Uttoxeter Road route was linked with Burton Road and this continued into the trolleybus era. An inspector talks to two crew members behind intending passengers who are all wearing hats. (Author's coll. Commercial postcard)

22.    Two passengers enjoy the afternoon sunshine and fresh air of a balcony seat in around 1906 on Car 30, destined for the Midland Station having arrived from Kedleston Road. It is about to enter St Peters Street, whilst Car 20 has a short distance to travel along the Cornmarket to the Market Place. Note the side destination board at the base of the middle lower deck window of car 30. (Author's coll. Commercial postcard)

# VICTORIA STREET

23.    Car 46 leaves Victoria Street and is about to enter the bottom of St Peters Street on its way to the Midland Station.  It was delivered in 1908 and the date on the postcard from which this view is taken is 1917.  In the distance is the dome of the one time Corn Exchange that opened in 1861 and doubled as a Palace Theatre of Varieties.  It subsequently became Northcliffe House, the home of the *Derby Evening Telegraph* before their move to The Meadows.  Note the advertisement for the Denby Kilburn Colliery Co Ltd on the end of the tram.  (Author's coll. Commercial postcard)

24.    Car 45 leaves Victoria Street on Route 2 to the Midland Station, having travelled from Ashbourne Road, and is about to enter the bottom of St Peters Street.  The tracks in the right foreground lead into the Cornmarket with the Royal Hotel and the Victoria Street Congregational Church in the background.  (Courtesy of Derby Museum & Art Gallery.  Ref. DMAG000221)

25.    The horse and dray make their way out of Victoria Street at the head of the Cornmarket, whilst Car 26 passes in the opposite direction on its way to Uttoxeter Road.  Side route indicators were introduced in 1913; judging from the dresses, this view was taken not long afterwards.  Note the stop sign in the foreground.  (W.W.Winter)

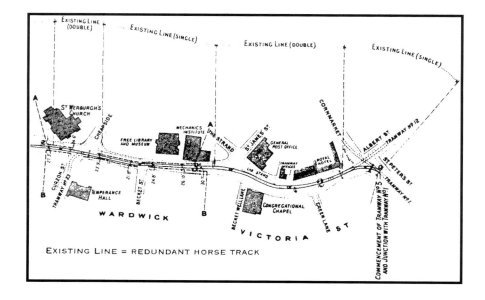

EXISTING LINE = REDUNDANT HORSE TRACK

26.     Three trams are seen in Victoria Street, with Car 56 in the foreground on Route 10, the Normanton/Pear Tree circular. In the background along Albert Street is the dome of Northcliffe House, the ex Corn Exchange and Palace Theatre. In the original proposals for the system, trams were planned to run along Albert Street, Morledge and Siddals Road to the Midland Station, but the tracks were never laid. The advent of traffic lights at the junction of Cornmarket and St Peters Street suggest an early 1930s view. (M.J.O'Connor via National Tramway Museum)

27.     A view in the early days of the system shows two cars waiting to depart from Victoria Street. Given that the motorman is at the controls of Car 3, the boom is swung round and positioned on the overhead furthest away, it is assumed it is about to depart for London Road and Alvaston. This poses the question as to the reason for the traditional British queue opposite the motorman with the boarding step folded in the up position. The shops to the left became Ranbys and subsequently, after rebuilding, the current Debenhams department store. (Author's coll. Commercial postcard)

28.　　A deserted Victoria Street is the backdrop to this view of Car 44 destined for Ashbourne Road. It was delivered in 1907 as an open top vehicle, but was given a top cover by Brush of Loughborough in 1913; driving protection has also been added. The Corporation Tramway Office building, which was built on the site of the old horse tramway company office and opened in 1904, is to the left and behind the front of 44. (A.D.Packer coll.)

29.　　Car 70 on Route 12 to Burton Road moves alongside the passenger shelter at the western end of Victoria Street in the late 1920s. 70 has arrived from Uttoxeter Road via the Wardwick which can be seen in the misty background (Courtesy of the *Derby Evening Telegraph*)

# WARDWICK/FRIARGATE/ASHBOURNE ROAD

30.     A busy scene in the Wardwick was recorded in around 1910 with Car 46 making its way along the interlaced track towards Victoria Street.  The Ashbourne Road and Uttoxeter Road routes used this short thoroughfare from Victoria Street before going their separate ways.  The Jacobean House on the corner of Beckett Street is on the right of the picture. (Author's coll. Commercial postcard)

31.     The view in the opposite direction shows Car 5 approaching the exit of the interlaced track as it makes its way towards Victoria Street.  There is a stop sign outside the railed Museum and Library premises on the right.  (W.W.Winter)

32.    Car 2 is about to pass under the second of the two bridges that had to be negotiated on the Derby system as it makes its way to Ashbourne Road in about 1910.  The graceful Friargate Bridge, produced by local iron founder Handyside, carried the Great Northern (later LNER) railway line into a station of the same name on the immediate left.  The horse tramway stables were under the railway arches on the right with the entrance to the covered yard on the other side of the bridge.  The Great Northern milk van on the bridge may be of interest to railway buffs.  (Author's coll.)

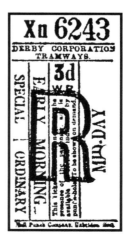

# SUPPLY AND ERECTION OF OVERHEAD EQUIPMENT.

| Number. | Description. | Rate. | Total. £ | s. | d. |
|---|---|---|---|---|---|
| 38 | Span wire suspensions, each consisting of 2 A poles and all span wire, insulators, ears, etc. | 16/17/4 | 641 | 8 | 2 |
| 10 | Span wire suspensions as above, but rosettes instead of poles | 3/11/7½ | 35 | 16 | 3 |
| 2 | Pull-off poles, complete | 9/16/4½ | 19 | 12 | 9 |
| 2 | Terminal poles, complete | 12/11/8 | 25 | 3 | 4 |
| 2 *m̃le* | Trolley wire ... *Per 100 yards* | 8/19/8-1 | 282 | 15 | 9 |
| 12 | Single pull-offs and necessary pull-off wire | 10/5½ | 6 | 5 | 6 |
| 12 | Double pull-offs and necessary pull-off wire | 13/5½ | 8 | 1 | 6 |
| 2 | Terminal clamps | 5/4 | | 10 | 8 |
| 6 | Section insulators | 1/17/9 | 11 | 6 | 6 |
| 2 | Frogs | 1/12/7 | 3 | 5 | 2 |
| 6 | Anchors | 17/3 | 5 | 3 | 6 |
| 1 | Crossing | | 1 | 12 | 7 |
| 1 mile | Guard wires, with all necessary bracket supports, etc., if required | | 28 | 2 | 10 |
| 85 | Excavations for poles and pillars | 6/ | 25 | 10 | 0 |
| 3 | Section boxes, complete | 24/18/9 | 74 | 16 | 3 |
| 950 | Bonds (ordinary) ... *Per 100* | 14/ | 133 | 0 | 0 |
| 150 | Cross Bonds ... " .. " | 22/9/11 | 33 | 14 | 10½ |
| 30 | Bonds, extra long, for special work .. " .. " | 65/12/6 | 19 | 13 | 4½ |
| | Include for carrying out the whole of the provisions of the Specification relating to above | | | | |
| | Allow for contingencies, to be deducted if not required | | 150 | 0 | 0 |
| | Allowance for telephones, etc. | | 10 | 0 | 0 |
| | Allowance for Evershed megger | | 20 | 0 | 0 |

*This tender is based on Electrolytic copper at £ 108:0:0 per ton and is subject to Market fluctuation.*

### Contract No. 9.
### Ashbourne Road Route.

TOTAL CARRIED TO SUMMARY    £1548 9 0

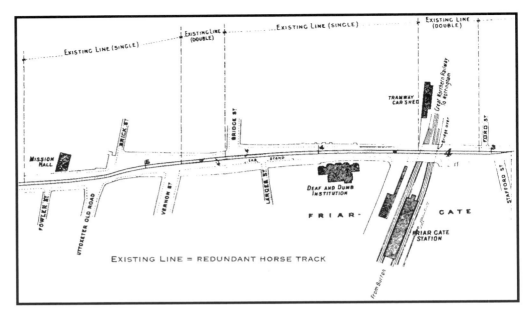

EXISTING LINE = REDUNDANT HORSE TRACK

33.     Car 13 leaves the Friargate Bridge behind and heads for Ashbourne Road.  The overhead was suspended by "Pringles Patent Tangential Suspension" on both this and the Uttoxeter Road routes and can be seen fitted from the span wires at the top of the picture.  Route number boxes have been added which puts the view post 1917/18.  (Author's coll. Commercial postcard)

4.     Ashbourne Road is viewed from the junction with Uttoxeter Old Road with a balcony car on
he outward journey to the terminus at the bottom of Windmill Hill Lane.
Author's coll. Commercial postcard)

# UTTOXETER ROAD

35.     Car 35 is about to turn right out of Curzon Street into the Wardwick in around 1910, having travelled the length of Uttoxeter Road.  St Werburghs Church is on the left, the Cathedral tower in the centre and the entrance to the Temperance Hall on the right. (Courtesy of Derby Museum & Art Gallery. Ref. DMAG000342)

36.  An unidentified car coasts down the gradua incline of Uttoxeter New Road, which is devoid of other traffic, as it makes its way to the Town The building on the left was originally a teacher training college with the girls' Practising Schoo next door.  The building is now used as a busines centre.

(Author's coll. Commercial postcard)

37.  Outward bound Car 19 reaches the Rowditch at the junction of Uttoxeter Old and New Roads the former descending the hill to the left.  Older local residents know this as Barracks Hill, presumably relating to the barracks of the Derbyshire Volunteer Rifle Corps built in the area during the late 1850's.  (Author's coll. Commercial postcard)

38.  Car 34 returns to town having left the passing loop at the end of Albany Road.  The track was eventually doubled between here and the terminus near to what is now the Manor Road/Kingsway junction with Uttoxeter Road.  Bemrose School, which opened in 1930, was built on land to the right of the picture.  (Don Gwinnett coll.)

41.    One of the single deck cars originally purchased for the Ashbourne Road route is seen in about 1925 halfway down St Peters Street. The Thurman and Malin department store is to the right of the car, as the four white coated gentlemen wheel their barrow of ladders down the hill presumably to the next painting assignment. (Author's coll.)

42.    Car 16, next to St Peters Church and on its way to Nottingham Road, is about to pass Car 25 whilst the telegram boy toils up the hill on his bicycle.  The road sweeper in front of the nearest car could well have doubled for Charlie Chaplin.  (Author's coll. Commercial postcard)

43.     Car 7 from the first delivery climbs St Peters Street across the St Peters Churchyard/East Street junction.  The trailing crossover in the foreground was used as the town terminus for the opening routes before work was completed on the track work and overhead into Victoria Street (Author's coll. Commercial postcard)

44.     Cars 11 and 32 have passed the crossover referred to in no. 43, as they descend St Peters Street to the Victoria Street/Cornmarket junction. Car 11 is from the original delivery of 1904 built by Brush, whilst Car 32, destined for the Market Place, was received in 1906 and built by Milnes Voss.  The presence of a pointsman at this crossover suggests it was still in use post 1906.  On the left is a dray belonging to White Brothers, purveyors of mineral water and ginger beer, who operated out of Havelock Road until late 2001.  It was pleasing to be able to add this view, taken between 1906 and 1910, to the company's memorabilia.  (Author's coll. Commercial postcard)

5.    This view, just below the Babington Lane junction, depicts Car 1 on Route 2 to Ashbourne Road from Midland Station. It is much rebuilt from its original open top and open platform design having had a roof provided via Brush in 1924 and then further modernised by the Corporation. The White Hall cinema, subsequently the Odeon, is to the right of the motorbike/sidecar and the "Magnet that draws the people" can be seen on top of the Midland Drapery store on the corner of East Street. (Author's coll. Commercial postcard)

6.    St Peters Street is decorated for a Royal Visit on 28th June 1906; two balcony cars are on view with the one on the left destined for Kedleston Road. There is no way of telling whether the photograph was taken before or after the visit but the two cars may be from the 30-35 batch newly into service on 1st June 1906, the same month of the Royal Visit. (Author's coll. Commercial postcard)

# BABINGTON LANE/BURTON ROAD

47.    Trolleybus overhead is in place in this view of Babington Lane with Car 70 using the positive wire whilst descending to St Peters Street. Both the Burton Road and Normanton routes used Babington Lane and they were converted to trolleybuses on 13th August 1933 and 18th March 1934 respectively; 70 was withdrawn shortly after the latter on 26th March. Motorbuses provided a service along Burton Road to Manor Road after the trams ceased on this route on 9th January 1932 and before trolleybuses commenced. It is assumed that the Guy motorbus outside the Grand Theatre is on this duty. (W.W.Winter)

48.    One of the original batch of cars is seen at the top of Babington Lane taking the track for Burton Road; the tracks in the foreground lead into Normanton Road. The background is the Babington Arms (licensee J Stanley), which dispensed Strettons Derby Ales, and whose maltings were in Surrey Street; Ind Coope & Allsop acquired the brewer in 1931. The scene is in the first few years of operation as indicated by the destination board fitted to the front dash. (J.S.Simnett)

49.    The conductor of Car 12 walks back after altering the points for the Burton Road route at the junction with Normanton Road. In later years major junctions were operated automatically. On the left is a circular cast iron gentleman's urinal and on the right are the properties of the "Little City" which fronted Burton Road. (Author's coll. Commercial postcard)

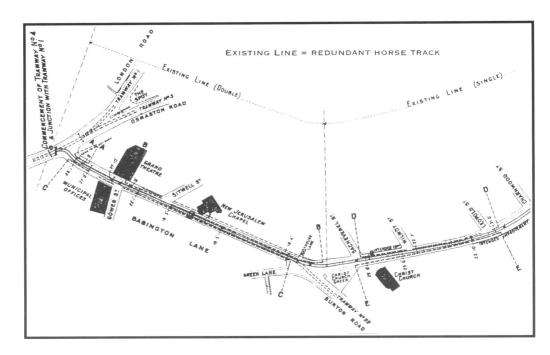

50.    Car 21 makes its way into town along Burton Road just above the junction with Abbey Street in around 1910 with period gas lamp in the foreground.  The steeply graded area to the right led up to the once privately owned Temple House which, in the author's childhood days, was the home of the dreaded school dentist.  (Author's coll. Commercial postcard)

1904

51.     The climb from Abbey Street was steeply graded and Car 11 is seen well patronised on the passing loop near Breedon Hill Road.  The destination is again shown on the front dash indicating the first few months of operation.  Bracket arm construction has been used for the overhead wiring, with the one in the foreground having two bracing supports and a guard wire. (W.W.Winter)

52.　The same location is seen with Car 19 inward bound for St Peters Street in about 1905. The houses on the right are easily recognisable today; immediately beyond is the Mount Carmel tower, which was in fact a chimney for Mason's paint works.
(Author's coll. Commercial postcard)

→

53.　An official photograph of the opening of the first stage of the Burton Road route as far as Vicarage Avenue on 8th September 1904. Two special cars were used including 19 on which the steepness of the staircase to the upper deck can be clearly seen; the ladies in their long Edwardian dresses must have found them difficult to negotiate. Also note the influence of a neighbouring city with the advertisement for the *Nottingham Daily Express*. (Author's coll.)

→

54.　The Burton Road route was extended to a point just beyond Whittaker Road on 30th July 1908 and Car 21 awaits departure to the Market Place from this terminus. (Barry Edwards coll.)

55.    Car 23 waits at the end of Normanton Road in 1904 to allow a traction engine to pass with its large load at the junction with Babington Lane on the right.  The Babington Arms is behind the traction engine and the Angel Inn (licensee Arthur Buxton) is on the left.  The houses and streets adjacent to The Angel were known as Little City comprising very basic workers' housing built around a silk mill in 1818/1819. (Author's coll. Commercial postcard)

56.    An animated scene in Normanton Roa with a car approaching the stop at the end Harriet Street on its way to the Cavendish in tl late 1920s.  The baby prams of the era certain lacked the "Silver Cross" styling. (Barry Edwards coll.)

57.    Towards the bottom of Normanton Road Car 10 waits for a lone passenger to board befor making its way to Victoria Street in about 1910.  The haberdashery and drapery store of Clark Pearce can be seen on the right with comprehensive window displays.  (W.W.Winter)

58.    Car 14 leaves the bottom of Normanton Road during the first two years of operation and climbs towards Rosehill Street with the towers of the Methodist and Congregational churches in the background.  Cast iron railings like those in front of the houses on the left were removed for scrap to help the War Effort during 1939-45. (Author's coll. Commercial postcard)

59.    The other "Five Lamps" at the junction of Normanton Road and Pear Tree Road with Car 17 moving into Lower Dale Road on its way to Upper Dale Road and the Cavendish.  These lamps did not carry their name over the generations unlike a similar structure at the Kedleston Road/Duffield Road junction. (J.S.Simnett)

60.    Two special cars, 7 and 19, were used to inaugurate the service to the Cavendish via Normanton Road on 8th September 1904, which was the same day as the Burton Road opening.  The party included the Mayor and the Tramway General Manager, F. Harding.  The Cavendish Hotel is on the left and in the distance across the fields and beyond the telegraph pole is the spire of St Giles Church, Normanton.  In the author's childhood days the building on the right was occupied by Bird's cake shop and bakery, the destination of a regular Saturday morning errand. (Author's coll.

61.    This early view looks along Upper Dale Road from the Cavendish in the first year after the route opened with the track finishing in the foreground.  The track was later extended around the corner to the right into Walbrook Road and along St Thomas Road to connect up with the track on Dairyhouse Road at The Vulcan.  This busy scene depicts Car 25 being prepared for the return journey to town.  (J.S.Simnett)

62. The Cavendish Hotel with Car 3 on the left at the end of Upper Dale Road, which was the original terminus, and Car 7 on the right at the end of Walbrook Road. The Victorian terraced houses of Walbrook Road stretch away towards St Thomas Road and The Vulcan; this section was opened on 5th September 1905 and the view taken not long afterwards.
(Courtesy of Derby Museum & Art Gallery.  Ref. DMAG001060)

**Normanton Road and Upper Dale Road Route.**

(Light—Orange).

WEEK-DAYS.

From Victoria Street to Cavendish, Upper Dale Road.

| Victoria St. | Norm'n H'l'l | Cavendish. | |
|---|---|---|---|
| Dep—a.m. | Dep—a.m. | Dep.—a.m. | to |
| 7 30 | 7 38 | 7 42 | Mid.Station |
| 7 45 | 7 53 | 7 57 | ,, |
| 8 0 | 8 8 | 8 12 | ,, |
| 8 6 | 8 14 | 8 18 | Circular |
| 8 12 | 8 20 | 8 24 | ,, |
| 8 18 | 8 26 | 8 30 | Mid. Stat'n. |
| 8 24 | 8 32 | 8 36 | Circular |
| 8 30 | 8 38 | 8 42 | Mid Stat'n. |
| 8 36 | 8 44 | 8 48 | Circular |
| 8 42 | 8 50 | 8 54 | Mid. Stat'n. |
| 8 48 | 8 56 | 9 0 | Circular |
| 8 54 | 9 2 | 9 6 | Mid. Stat'n. |
| 9 0 | 9 8 | 9 12 | Circular |
| and every 6 minutes until | | | |
| 11 6 | 11 14 | 11 18 | To Depot |
| p.m. | p.m. | p.m. | |
| Saturdays until | | | |
| p.m. | p.m. | p.m. | |
| 11 12 & | 11 20 & | 11 24 & | To Depot |
| 11 18 | 11 26 | 11 30 | |

The 8.12 a.m. and every alternate Car is a Circular Car via Douglas Street and Osmaston Road. The 8.18 a.m. and every alternate Car until 10.42 from Victoria Street; 10.50 Normanton Hotel and 10.57 Car runs through to Midland Station.

NORMANTON ROAD & UPPER DALE ROAD ROUTE.—*contd.*

(Light—Orange).

WEEK-DAYS.

Cavendish to Town.

| Cavendish. | Normant'n Htl. | Victoria St. |
|---|---|---|
| Dep.—a.m. | Dep.—a.m. | Arr.—a.m. |
| 7 45 | 7 49 | 7 57 |
| 8 0 | 8 4 | 8 12 |
| 8 15 | 8 19 | 8 27 |
| 8 21 | 8 25 | 8 33 |
| 8 27 | 8 31 | 8 39 |
| 8 33 | 8 37 | 8 45 |
| 8 39 | 8 43 | 8 51 |
| 8 45 | 8 49 | 8 57 |
| 8 51 | 8 55 | 9 3 |
| 8 57 | 9 1 | 9 9 |
| 9 3 | 9 7 | 9 15 |
| 9 9 | 9 13 | 9 21 |
| and every 6 minutes until 1 9, then | | |
| p.m. | p.m. | p.m. |
| 1 12 | 11 17 | 1 27 |
| 1 18 | 1 23 | 1 33 |
| 1 24 | 1 29 | 1 39 |
| and every 6 minutes until | | |
| 11 18 | 11 23 | 11 33 |
| Saturdays until | | |
| 11 24 | 11 29 | 11 39 |
| 11 30 | 11 35 | 11 45 |
| p.m. | p.m. | p.m. |

1904

# ST THOMAS ROAD/DAIRYHOUSE ROAD/DOUGLAS STREET

63.    Car 30, seen at the end of Dairyhouse Road, is about to enter St Thomas Road. The Vulcan public house is to the right of the photographer's position; this was the Pear Tree destination with Pear Tree Road to the left and Princes Street to the right.   The Normanton Picture Palace, which was opened in March 1913, was a regular haunt during the author's childhood days in the 1940s.
(Author's coll. Commercial postcard)

64.    Dairyhouse Road in around 1912 is deserted, apart from Car 50 which is about to leave the passing loop and climb the hill to St James' Church and thence into Douglas Street. The track was doubled in 1927. The road crossing in the foreground is Cambridge Street with the Cambridge Hotel on the left and the access towards the Baseball Ground, former home of Derby County, on the right.
(Author's coll.)

65.    Car 18 descends Douglas Street towards Osmaston Road having just moved onto single track after leaving the passing loop by St James' Church around 1907 and having climbed Dairyhouse Road from The Vulcan. (Courtesy of Derby Museum & Art Gallery.  Ref. DMAG001070)

# THE SPOT

66.    A busy scene at The Spot has two cars at the entrance to Osmaston Road with London Road to the left of the Freeman Hardy and Willis shop. Car 42 on the right was delivered in 1907 and received a roof via Brush in 1913. Queen Victoria's statue was unveiled in 1906 by King Edward VII and was subsequently moved to the grounds of the Derbyshire Royal Infirmary. (Author's coll. Commercial postcard)

67.    Cars 8 and 23 are on the London Road leg of The Spot shortly after the opening of the system, with destination boards hung from the dash - this was a carry over from the horse tram days. It appears that the conductor of 23 had forgotten to change the indicator as it is still showing Midland Railway Station. The building to the left of Harrisons is the Cheshire Cheese public house. (W.W.Winter)

68.    At the same location a car from the 30-35 batch is about to move along London Road to Alvaston with the motorman looking over his shoulder to check progress on loading. It is a sunny day post 1929 and a few passengers have taken balcony seats at both ends. Note the four bay upper deck construction compared with the three bay lower deck.
(W. Gratwicke via Science Museum. Ref. W6248)

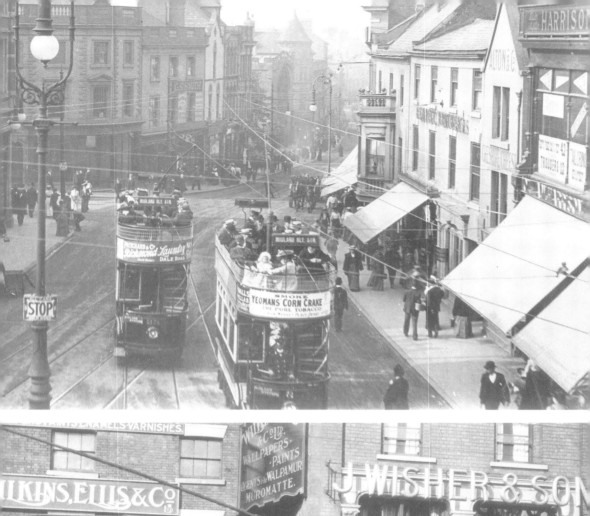

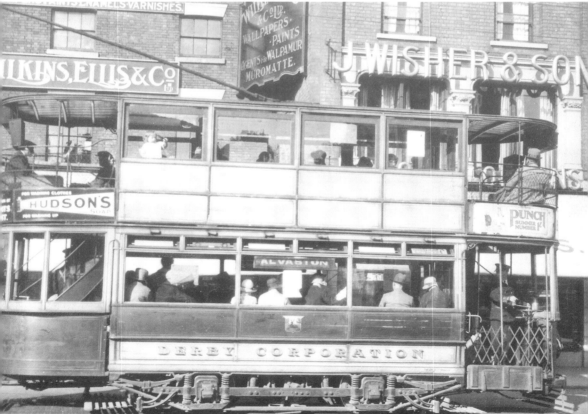

69.    One of the single deck cars purchased to pass under Friargate railway bridge, although the road was lowered for double deckers prior to the route opening, is seen on a short working to Brighton Road on the Alvaston route. This view provides a good side elevation showing the clerestory roof.
(W. Gratwicke via Science Museum. Ref. W6239)

70.    Car 49, delivered in 1911, leaves The Spot to descend St Peters Street to the Market Place on Route 4 from Alvaston post 1929. Although the advertisement for "His Master's Voice" appears to be mounted on the roof of 49, it was above the premises of J Wisher & Son a supplier of musical instruments and sheet music. (W Gratwicke via Science Museum. Ref. W6247)

71.    A busy scene in about 1930 on the London Road leg of The Spot has five trams in view showing the development in design starting with an open top version in the foreground; next comes a covered car but with open balcony and a fully enclosed car is in the rear. The open top car is 18 from the original delivery, but with the platform now enclosed, followed by 55 delivered in 1920. (Author's coll.)

# LONDON ROAD/MIDLAND STATION/ALVASTON

72.    A few hundred yards along London Road from The Spot, Car 7 is seen outside the railings fronting the Congregational Church with the Temperance Hotel above The West End Store immediately beyond. The dash destination again indicates a view taken in the early months after the opening of the system.  The church later became the Coliseum Cinema. (Author's coll.)

73.    Cars 2 and 17 from the first delivery proceed in opposite directions in about 1910 on a wider section of London Road outside the grounds of the Derbyshire Royal Infirmary on the right. The wider road allowed the erection of centre bracket arm supports for the overhead, although these were removed and replaced by span wires in 1911.
(Author's coll. Commercial postcard)

74.    Outside the gates of the Derbyshire Royal Infirmary in around 1908, Car 14 pauses at the stop sign prior to completing its journey to the Midland Station.  Closer examination reveals quite an animated scene with many unaccompanied children in view. (Author's coll. Commercial postcard)

75.    Inward bound Car 19 overtakes a dray as it approaches the Infirmary entrance in the first year of operation with the ghostly profile of St Andrews Church in the background.
(Author's coll. Commercial postcard)

76.    Car 34, produced by Milnes Voss and delivered in 1906, makes its way along London Road towards town and thence on to Kedleston Road. Immediately in front of 34 is the tower of Holy Trinity Church, whilst the Queen's Hall Methodist Church is in the centre of the picture. Of interest is the Cosy Picture House on the extreme right complete with commissionaire in full uniform; it was opened in 1913 and by the time it closed in 1959 it had become The Cameo. The change to span wire suspension of the overhead can be clearly seen in this view.
(Author's coll. Commercial postcard)

57.     Turning now towards the Midland Station this view looks down Midland Road around 1908, with Car 41, destined for Ashbourne Road, advancing towards the London Road junction, with the station façade in the background. Judging by the window boxes and shop window sun blinds, this view was taken on a warm summer's day. (Author's coll. Commercial postcard)

78.    A wonderful period view from about 1914 looking along Midland Road from London Road
with balcony Car 34 making its way to Midland Station.  Car 22 is about to turn to its left into
London Road on its way to the Cavendish.  The building with three arched ground floor windows on
the right houses the business of W.W.Winter, a Victorian photographer who took many early street
scenes of Derby; the business still continues to trade.  Note the suspended pendant street lamp.
(W.W.Winter)

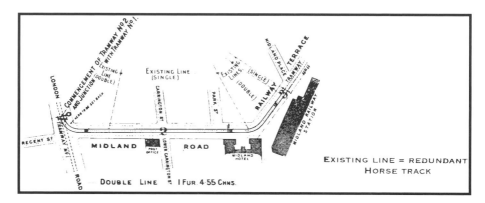

9.    A late 1920s view of Midland Road with an unidentified fully enclosed car (possibly 68)
aking its way to the London Road junction.  A sign of how times have changed is indicated by the
ck of any horse drawn traffic.  The Post Office to the right of the tram was the site of the original
orse tram depot which came into use in 1880.  (W.W.Winter)

80.　Car 74 from the final batch of trams delivered in 1927 has almost reached its Midland Station destination having arrived via Normanton Road, Cavendish and Pear Tree. The photograph is dated 25th June 1933, by which time trolleybus overhead had been erected which can be seen taking a left hand turn into Park Street for the "round the houses" loop to reach the station forecourt stand. Car 74 will however carry straight on before turning left into Railway Terrace. A Trent single decker bus completes the picture. (H.C.Casserley)

81.　A busy scene outside Midland Station in the months immediately after the opening of the system as indicated by the destination of London Road and Alvaston displayed on Car 18; this service was discontinued on 23rd September 1904. The station buildings were erected over a number years by the Midland Railway in the 19th century and were swept away in 1985 to be replaced by the current station façade. The local carrier to Shardlow and Castle Donington awaits custom.
(Author's coll. Commercial postcard)

82.　Car 55 from the 1920 delivery waits outside the Midland Station forecourt for a journey to Ashbourne Road. The motorman appears to be walking round the front to pick up a package for delivery en route. It looks like a lawnmower grassbox perhaps a product of Qualcast who, at the time this photograph was taken in about 1928, occupied Derwent Foundry which was on the site of the current Exeter House flats opposite the River Gardens. (R.Wilson)

83.    Car 64, delivered in 1925, awaits departure to Kedleston Road on the Monday-Saturday
Route 1 from a wet deserted station forecourt.  The building on the right is the Midland Hotel
opened in 1841.  (Author's coll.)

| Xu6586 | | |
|---|---|---|
| DERBY CORPORATION TRAMWAYS | | |
| Victoria Street | 1½d | Caven- dish |
| | Nton. | |
| Moore Street | | Cam- bridge St |
| Caven- dish | | Arbore- tum St |
| Caven- dish | | Midland Station |
| Vulcan (Pear Tree) | | Vict. Street |
| To Car Depot | | From Car Depot |

This Ticket must be punched in the presence of the passenger and is available in section indicated by punch-hole.  To be shown on demand.

84.    This view from around 1905 depicts Car 21 unloading in front of Midland Station having arrived from Pear Tree.  It will move forward and cross onto the right hand track before moving back to a position opposite the stop sign ready for the return journey.  Note the horse drawn "taxis" in the right hand background.  (Author's coll. Commercial postcard)

85.   Single deck Car 36, returning to Osmaston Road car depot, awaits the departure of Car 29 on Route 2 to Ashbourne Road. The single decker is showing Route 4 Market Place to Alvaston so why it should be outside the Midland Station is not apparent. Perhaps it is awaiting football supporters for the journey to the Baseball Ground, erstwhile home of Derby County. (G.N.Southerden)

86.   Track in front of the station forecourt extended a short distance along Railway Terrace to provide parking for layovers and workman specials for the Midland Railway Locomotive Works which could be accessed by a footbridge across the station platforms and avoiding lines. This car from the original delivery, but rebuilt to fully enclosed specification, is seen in the layover siding with the side indicator set for Ashbourne Road as the motorman swings the boom around ready for the next trip. (Author's coll.)

87.   Returning now to London Road, Car 49 is seen in about 1930 at the junction with Midland Road as it makes its way to Alvaston on Route 4. (Author's coll.)

88. The graceful lines of St Andrews Church dominate this view of Car 4 at the junction of Midland Road and London Road. Judging by the clothes and hats the period is early 1900s and the umbrella on the front upper deck suggests a warm summer's day. St Andrews was the "Railwaymen's Church" and was built to the design of Gilbert Scott who was also retained by the Midland Railway for the design of St Pancras Station in London. (J.S.Simnett)

89. One of the original delivery of open top cars is on a short working to Brighton Road. The location is again the junction with Midland Road and the clothes suggest a late 1920s view. Note the advertisement for the Derby Daily Telegraph and the lattice gate preventing intending passengers boarding the motorman's platform. (W. Gratwicke via Science Museum Ref. W6240)

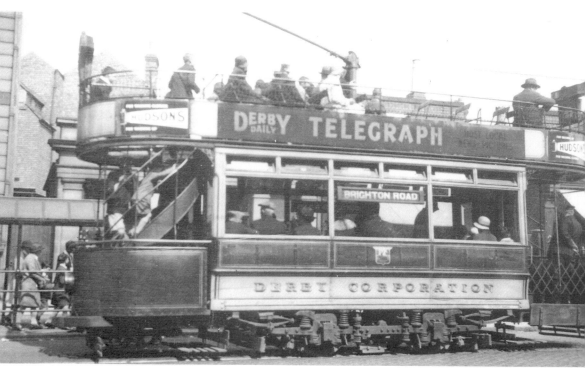

0.    Victorian terraced houses adjacent to Rugby Street form the background to this view of Car 6 delivered in 1905 as it makes it way along London Road to the humpback bridge over the Derby anal immediately before the Brighton Road short working terminus.  The then Mission Church is n the left.  (Author's coll. Commercial postcard)

1.    The Harrington Arms was the terminus of the Alvaston route.  Car 8, complete with dash idicator board showing the short lived 1904 route to Midland Station, pulls to a halt whilst Edwardian adies prepare to board.  The railings on the right fronted the grounds of the Derby Laundry Company; ie site is now a row of shops.  (J.S.Simnett)

92.      This is a second view of the Alvaston terminus, but viewed from the opposite direction.  The crew of Car 11 pose for the photographer prior to returning to the Market Place against a background that is unrecognisable today.  London Road continues to the right in what is now a dual carriageway with shops on either side.  A traffic island occupies the area where the houses stand; the sign over the doorway indicates "G Holmes House Painter". (Author's coll. Commercial postcard)

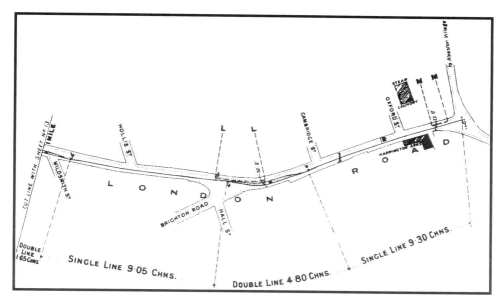

93.    A further posed view at the same location was taken in the summer of 1906 and probably when Car 34 was newly into service in June. Note the route indicator board at the bottom of the centre lower deck window. Raynesway now runs to the left of this view and the signboard in the background directs intending worshippers "To the Alvaston Baptist Church".
(Author's coll. Commercial postcard)

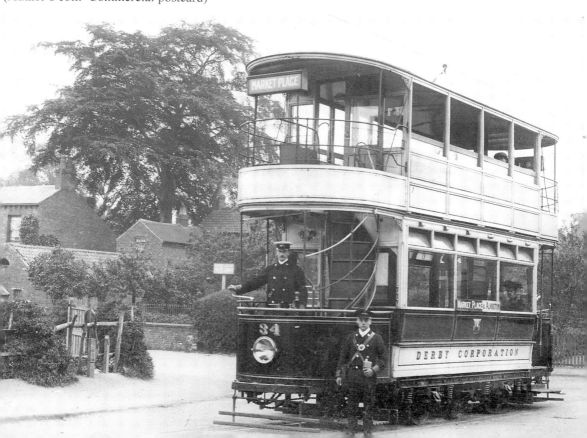

94.    Car 21 is working wrong line in Osmaston Road. Something is amiss, as the conductor is standing chatting to a pedestrian. Passing on the right is a horse bus carrying what appears to be fleet number 22. It was one of a number purchased from the Manchester Carriage & Tramways Company in 1903.
(Author's coll. Commercial postcard)

95.    Car 7 makes its way along Osmaston Road near Melbourne Street inward bound for the Market Place and thence onward to Nottingham Road sometime between 1908 when the latter route was opened and 1917/18 when route number boxes were introduced. The cyclist makes sure he keeps between the tramlines. (W.W.Winter)

96.    Car 22 is seen again, this time on Osmaston Road near Hartington Street in around 1905, with the spire of the Baptist Church in the background. It looks as if the trees on the right need cutting back if they are not to interfere with the upper deck passengers and the bracket arm suspended overhead. (Author's coll. Commercial postcard)

97.     Edwardian schoolboys look at the photographer taking this shot of Car 24 in Osmaston Road near Grove Street on its way to town and with no other vehicle in sight.  The property in this view has all disappeared together with the section of Grove Street that joined Osmaston Road. (Author's coll.)

1904

### Osmaston Road Route.

(Blue Light).

MONDAYS, TUESDAYS, WEDNESDAYS, THURSDAYS, AND FRIDAYS.

| Cars leave Victoria Street every 15 minutes from 8 a.m. to 11 p.m. | Cars leave Cotton Lane every 15 minutes from 7.45 a.m. to 10.45 p.m. |

SATURDAYS.

| Cars leave Victoria Street every 15 minutes from 8 a.m. to 12 noon, and from 12 noon to 11 p.m. every 10 minutes | Cars leave Cotton Lane every 15 minutes from 7.45 a.m. to 12 noon, & from 12.15 p.m. to 11 p.m. every 10 minutes |

SUNDAYS.

| Cars leave Victoria Street every 15 minutes from 2 p.m. to 10.15 p.m. | Cars leave Cotton Lane every 15 minutes from 1.45 to 10.0 p.m. |

*Fares*, 1d. each, either way.

STOPPING PLACES.

Victoria Street, St. Peter's Street, St. Peter's Church, The Spot, Sacheverel Street, Charnwood Street, Hartington Street, Grove Street, Regent Street, High Street, Reginald Street, Bateman Street, Douglas Street, Shaftesbury Street, Litchurch Lane, Russell Street, Graham Street, Terminus.

8.   Car 8 pauses at the stop opposite the end of Bateman Street in about 1919 on its way along smaston Road to the town centre and then onwards to Nottingham Road. Bateman Street is to the ght behind the little girl in white and the Rolls-Royce Club site is behind the wall beyond. Author's coll.  Commercial postcard)

| Xo 9203 | | |
|---|---|---|
| DERBY   CORPORATION TRAMWAYS. | | |
| Osmaston Park Road | 1½d | Arboretum Street ) |
| Nightin- gale Road | Osm. | Mark Place |
| Arboretum Street | | Stores Road |
| Royal Hotel | | Notting- ham Road |
| Uttoxeter Road | | Victoria Street |
| Boundary Road | | Abbey St (Top |
| Victoria Street | | Burton Road |
| Victoria Street | | Old Ches- ter Road |
| Derwent St Nott'm Rd End) | | Darley Abbey Lane |
| To Car Depot | | From Car Depot |

99.    A view from the rear upper deck of a tram outward bound along Osmaston Road with Car 77 passing what is now Ivy Square.  The tracks on the left lead into Douglas Street and notes with the photograph suggests the car in the foreground is taking the then Chief Constable to the Rolls-Royce factory on the occasion of a visit by the Prince of Wales in June 1932. (C.Shepperd. Courtesy of Derby Museum & Art Gallery. Ref. DMAG001062)

100.    At the Shaftsbury Street stop th motorman watches the departing ladies who loo as if they have left Car 25 by the front platform emphasised by the fact the folding step is down In the background are the W & T Fletcher Sil Mills; Derby County may well be playing a home judging by the gentleman in the scarf o the right.
(M.J.O'Connor via National Tramway Museum

101.    The conductor of Car 60 swings the boom around ready to take up service on Route 11, th Normanton circular outward via Osmaston Road, having moved out from the Osmaston Road depo on the left.  In the past there had been much debate as to whether this was just a parking siding on th Osmaston Road depot site, but research by Barry Edwards has shown conclusively that the ex foundry building was used as a covered depot.  Note the advertisements on the end wall of th Carriage & Wagon Works. (M.J.O'Connor via National Tramway Museum)

102.    The track in the foreground of this photo from about 1930 leads into the Abingdon Street
depot and works.  Car 25 is again on view in original bodywork condition apart from the addition o
route number boxes and side route indicators.  Car 25 is about to enter the depot, the conducto
having changed the points ready for this manoeuvre.  This was the end of the line for the Osmasto
Road route until the 1923 extension to near the junction with Osmaston Park Road.  The LMS (e
Midland Railway) Carriage & Wagon Works are in the background.
(M.J.O'Connor via National Tramway Museum)

# DEPOTS & WORKSHOPS

103.   The forecourt of Abingdon Street depot in June 1932 with Car 77 from the last delivery in 1927 amongst the track splays leading into the depot buildings.  Car 5 stands on the left in a somewhat dilapidated state; by this time it was used on service support duties mainly for towing an ex-horse drawn car for the application of sand and salt to the track when conditions dictated.  (R.Wilson)

104.    Another view of Abingdon Street depot shows the three bay construction and with Car 52 on the right.  The two bays on the right and the out of view workshop were the first to be built and opened in 1904 with the Paint Shop at the rear of the bay on the extreme right.  The left hand bay was an extension built in 1906/07; this was allowed for in the original plan for the site.  This depot was subsequently used as a workshop for the trolleybus and motorbus fleets and was vacated operationally in 1950.  (R.Wilson)

———————➤

105.    This rather poor view is the only one that has come to light of the second depot in Osmaston Road used in the tramway era.  It was opened in 1928 possibly in anticipation of a lack of tram access over the new Exeter River Bridge and because of the growing motorbus fleet.  The buildings had previously been owned by Swinglers Foundry, and prior to that, the Victoria & Railway Iron Works.  Car 50 can be seen about to cross the points of the track leading into the depot yard.  Access to the depot building was out of view on the left.  The tram section of the depot was gradually changed over to trolleybuses by the mid 1930s as their ever increasing numbers, and hence declining numbers of trams outgrew the accommodation at Nottingham Road.  (M.J.O'Connor via National Tramway Museum)

———————➤

106.    No picture has been found of Nottingham Road depot when operational with trams so this view has been included which was taken in 1995; the premises had been vacated by the Omnibus Department in 1949.  The four nearest bays were opened on 1st February 1909 and extended in 1926. With the 1931 opening of Exeter Bridge over the River Derwent, there was no tram access to the depot, although track had been laid on one half of the bridge during construction to allow the facility to be used well into 1930.  It was adapted for trolleybuses ready for the conversion programme with the Nottingham Road route being the first to operate.  (P.J.Thomas)

107.   The men behind the scenes.  A group of tradesmen, all wearing caps, stand beside a car from the original delivery in the forecourt of Abingdon Street depot.  The photograph, taken prior to 1915, may well have been commissioned to illustrate the greenhouse like vestibules which had been erected to provide motorman weather protection.  An interesting point is the absence of route indicator boxes at each end of the upper deck.  The entrance to the depot yard on the corner of Abingdon Street can be seen on the right.  (Author's coll. Commercial postcard)

| Vz **3389** | | |
|---|---|---|
| DERBY CORPORATION TRAMWAYS. | | |
| Osmaston Park Road | 1½d | Arboretum Street |
| Nightingale Road | Osm. | Market Place |
| Arboretum Street | | Stores Road |
| Royal Hotel | | Nottingham Road |
| Uttoxeter Road | | Victoria Street |
| Boundary Road | | Abbey St. (Top) |
| Victoria Street | | Burton Road |
| Mansfield Road | | Centre |
| City Road | | Uttoxeter Old Road |
| Wardwick | | Mackenzie Street |
| Bell Punch Co., Uxbridge. 111 | | |

This Ticket must be punched in the presence of the passenger, and is available in section indicated by punch-hole. To be shown on demand

# ROLLING STOCK

## Cars 1-25 (1903/4)

08. This was the initial batch of cars delivered for the opening of the system. Cars 1 and 2 arrived in December 1903 and were used, together with subsequent deliveries, for driver training until the majority were available for the system opening on 26th July 1904. They were produced by Brush of Loughborough being fitted with their own design of truck, two BTH GE52 25HP motors GE K10 controllers and 48 seat open top body. 1/3/4/8/9/22/23 were rebuilt as fully enclosed by the Corporation between 1922 and 1927. Brush supplied the roof covers and at the same time the department rebuilt the trucks to 7'0" (2133 mm). It is thought several other trucks were also modified in the same way. The alternative suggestion that almost the entire batch received replacement Brill trucks is not supported by photographic evidence. Cars 5 and 24 were used as works cars in later years and the whole batch were withdrawn between 1928 and 1933 with the majority going in 1932/3. Cars 7 and 21 are seen outside Abingdon Street depot. (Author's coll.)

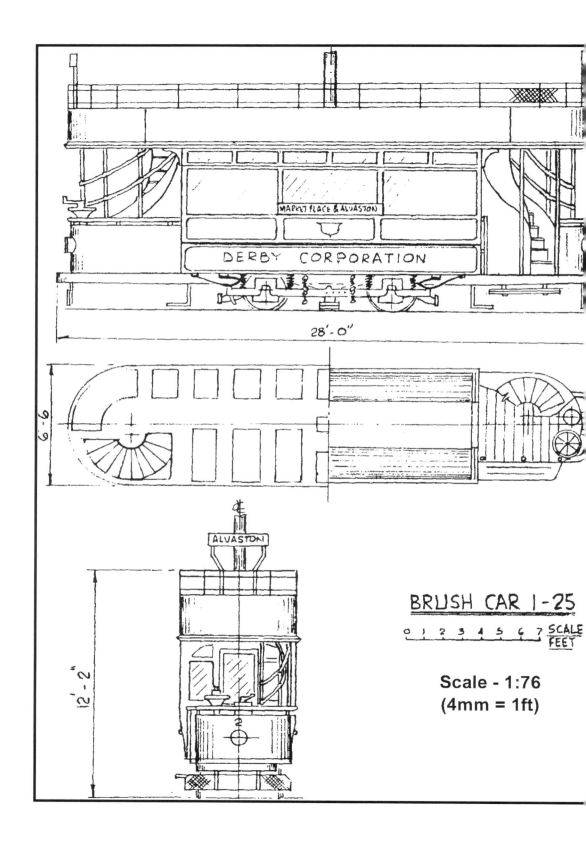

28'- 0"

6' - 9"

MARKET PLACE & ALVASTON

DERBY CORPORATION

ALVASTON

12' - 2"

BRUSH CAR 1-25

0 1 2 3 4 5 6 7 SCALE
FEET

Scale - 1:76
(4mm = 1ft)

## Cars 26-29 (1905)

109.    The second delivery was also Brush built with two BTH GE52 25HP motors, Lycett & Conaty radial 5'6" trucks (1676mm), GE K10 controllers and 48 seat covered balcony bodies.  They were retrucked with Peckham P22 7'6" (2286mm) trucks in 1925/26 and were withdrawn in 1932.  Car 27 is depicted in about 1906.
(Don Gwinnett coll. Commercial postcard)

## Cars 30-35 (1906)

110.    A change of supplier saw the next six cars being produced by Milnes Voss of Birkenhead and fitted with two BTH GE52 25HP motors, M & G 8'6" (2591mm) trucks, GE K10 controllers and 52 seat covered balcony bodies.  They were retrucked with Peckham P22 7'6" (2286mm) trucks in 1920/21, and were withdrawn in 1933.
(Author's coll.  Commercial postcard)

## Cars 36-39 (1906)

111.    Four single deck cars, also produced by Milnes Voss, were purchased from an initial order for seven vehicles to pass under the Friargate railway bridge, but with the lowering of the road to allow double deck cars to pass they tended to be used on peak hour and duplicate duties particularly on short workings to Brighton Road on the Alvaston route.  They had two BTH GE52 25HP motors, M & G 8'6" (2591mm) radial trucks, GE K10 controllers and single deck bodies seating 32 with 30 inside the saloon and 2 technically outside on the non-driving end.  Note the clerestory roof and the curtains in this view of Car 38 in the forecourt of Abingdon Street depot.  They were withdrawn in 1932.  (D.C.O.D.)

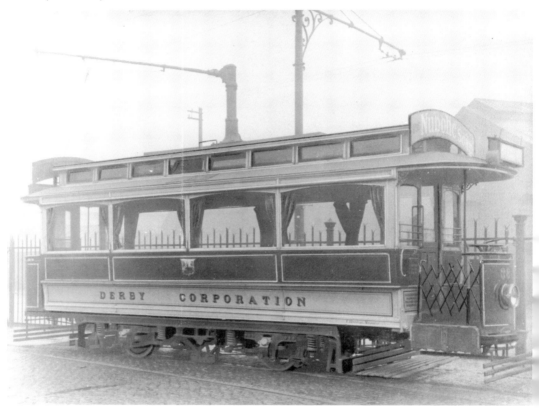

## Cars 40-41 (1907)

112.     These two cars were unusual in that they were fitted with short bodies at only 12'6" (3810mm) between bulkheads; they were taken, together with 43-45, in lieu of the cancelled order for three single deckers.  They were produced by Milnes Voss with two BTH GE52 25HP motors, M & G 21EM 5'6" (1676mm) trucks, GE K10 controllers and open top 42 seat bodies.  They were fitted with roofs via Brush in 1913 and were withdrawn in 1930 and 1932 respectively.  One of the cars is seen on the south side of the Market Place in about 1930 with added motorman weather protection. (Author's coll.)

## Cars 42-44 (1907)

113.    These three cars were part of the same delivery from Milnes Voss and were fitted with two of the by now standard BTH 25HP motors (GE54), M & G radial 8'6" (2591mm) trucks, GE K10 controllers and 52 seat open top bodies.  Roofs via Brush were added in 1913 and Peckham P22 7'6" (2286mm) trucks fitted in 1921.  They were withdrawn at the end of 1933.  Car 43 is seen outside the Midland Station forecourt.  (Author's coll. Commercial postcard)

## Cars 45-47 (1908)

14.    The next three cars were also from Milnes Voss.  All were fitted with BTH motors (two G54 5HP and one GE200 30HP), M & G 21EM 5'6" (1676mm) trucks, GE K10 controllers and 52 seat open top bodies.  Brush built roofs were fitted during 1914/18 and the cars were retrucked with Peckham P22 7'6" (2286mm) trucks in 1921.  47 was withdrawn in 1931 and the remainder in 1933. Car 46 picks up passengers on the London Road leg of The Spot. (M.J.O'Connor via National Tramway Museum)

## Cars 48-50 (1911)

15.    The three year gap in deliveries saw a return to Brush for the next three cars.  The trial with the BTH G200 motors in the previous delivery must have been successful as these 30HP motors were specified for this order.  Brush Flexible 7'6" (2286mm) trucks were fitted with 52 seat covered balcony bodies and GE K10 controllers.  They were withdrawn in 1933.  Car 48 is seen opposite the Osmaston Road depot. (M.J.O'Connor via National Tramway Museum)

## Cars 51-56 (1920)
## Cars 57-60 (1921)

*(left)* 116.    There was a nine year gap, which covered the period of the First World War, before there were further deliveries in 1920 and 1921.  The orders were awarded to Brush and the BTH G200 30HP motors fitted together with Peckham P22 7'6" (2286mm) trucks and GE K10 controllers. Covered 52 seat balcony style bodies with fully enclosed platforms were fitted; Car 57 was withdrawn in 1932 and the remainder in 1934.  Car 53 is pictured in the parking spur in Railway Terrace.  (W. Gratwicke via Science Museum. Ref. W6246)

## Cars 61-66 (1925)
## Cars 67-72 (1926)
## Cars 73-78 (1927)

*(lower left)* 117. The next eighteen cars were all basically the same design from Brush, the Corporation having standardised on the BTH G200 30HP motor and Peckham P22 7'6" (2286mm) truck.  Covered fully enclosed 52 seat bodies were fitted together with GE K10 controllers and all were withdrawn after a short life with the closure of the system in 1934.  Special Board of Trade permission had to be obtained to allow fully enclosed cars on four wheels to run on the 4' 0" (1219mm) gauge and eighteen of the last twenty-eight cars had their controllers changed to B510 around 1927/28.  The motorman of Car 73 lifts up the pivoting step recently used by exiting passengers as he gets his driving position arranged ready for the departure from Railway Terrace.  (Author's coll.)

# TOWER WAGONS

118.    Overhead wiring is receiving attention in St Peters Street just below The Spot with tower wagon CH1812 in attendance.  This vehicle was originally single deck GMC-Edison battery bus 2 delivered late in 1919 and put into service January 1920.  It was purchased for the Mansfield Road route and converted into a tower wagon in 1924 and eventually withdrawn in 1931.  There was also another original Edison battery tower wagon CH1134 delivered in 1914.  In this view Car 51 is about to descend St Peters Street on its way to Kedleston Road with a much rebuilt Car 4 on the extreme right.  (Author's coll.)

# THE BEGINNING AND THE END

119.    This six-car line up has worked wrong line towards town to reach a position in London Road near Bradshaw Street ready for the official opening of the electric tramway system on the afternoon on 27th July 1904. Car 3 is heavily decorated for the Mayor and dignitaries with the remainder of the party in the other cars. They moved to a position between The Spot and Castle Street, the booms turned 180 degrees and Car 3 then led the procession along London Road to the Alvaston terminus before returning as far as Bateman Street. The procession then proceeded along this thoroughfare to reach Osmaston Road. From here they travelled along Osmaston Road to the end of the line at the Abingdon Street depot where the Mayor hosted a reception before the cars returned the participants to town. Public services commenced at 6.00pm. (J.S.Simnett)

20.    The official end to the tramway system was 2<sup>nd</sup> July 1934, although last duties had finished on 30<sup>th</sup> June.  The last delivered Car 78 poses in Victoria Street with Guy trolleybus 127 in the background.  So ended almost 30 years of railed electric public transport, which included the difficult First World War years, but electric traction was to continue for another 33 years with the replacement trolleybuses.  (Courtesy of the *Derby Evening Telegraph*)

# MP Middleton Press

Easebourne Lane, Midhurst, W Sussex. GU29 9AZ Tel: 01730 813169 Fax: 01730 812601
Email: sales@middletonpress.co.uk   www.middletonpress.co.uk
*If books are not available from your local transport stockist, order direct post free UK.*

## BRANCH LINES
Branch Line to Allhallows
Branch Line to Alton
Branch Lines around Ascot
Branch Line to Ashburton
Branch Lines around Bodmin
Branch Line to Bude
Branch Lines around Canterbury
Branch Lines around Chard & Yeovil
Branch Line to Cheddar
Branch Lines around Cromer
Branch Line to the Derwent Valley
Branch Lines to East Grinstead
Branch Lines of East London
Branch Lines to Effingham Junction
Branch Lines around Exmouth
Branch Lines to Falmouth, Helston & St. Ives
Branch Line to Fairford
Branch Lines to Felixstow & Aldeburgh
Branch Lines around Gosport
Branch Line to Hayling
Branch Lines to Henley, Windsor & Marlow
Branch Line to Hawkhurst
Branch Line to Horsham
Branch Lines around Huntingdon
Branch Line to Ilfracombe
Branch Line to Kingsbridge
Branch Line to Kingswear
Branch Line to Lambourn
Branch Lines to Launceston & Princetown
Branch Lines to Longmoor
Branch Line to Looe
Branch Line to Lyme Regis
Branch Line to Lynton
Branch Lines around March
Branch Lines around Midhurst
Branch Line to Minehead
Branch Line to Moretonhampstead
Branch Lines to Newport (IOW)
Branch Lines to Newquay
Branch Lines around North Woolwich
Branch Line to Padstow
Branch Lines to Princes Risborough
Branch Lines to Seaton and Sidmouth
Branch Lines around Sheerness
Branch Line to Shrewsbury
Branch Line to Tenterden
Branch Lines around Tiverton
Branch Lines to Torrington
Branch Lines to Tunbridge Wells
Branch Line to Upwell
Branch Lines of West London
Branch Lines of West Wiltshire
Branch Lines around Weymouth
Branch Lines around Wimborne
Branch Lines around Wisbech

## NARROW GAUGE
Austrian Narrow Gauge
Branch Line to Lynton
Branch Lines around Portmadoc 1923-46
Branch Lines around Porthmadog 1954-94
Branch Line to Southwold
Douglas to Port Erin
Douglas to Peel
Kent Narrow Gauge
Northern France Narrow Gauge
Romneyrail
Southern France Narrow Gauge
Sussex Narrow Gauge
Surrey Narrow Gauge
Swiss Narrow Gauge

Two-Foot Gauge Survivors
Vivarais Narrow Gauge

## SOUTH COAST RAILWAYS
Ashford to Dover
Bournemouth to Weymouth
Brighton to Worthing
Dover to Ramsgate
Eastbourne to Hastings
Hastings to Ashford
Portsmouth to Southampton
Ryde to Ventnor
Southampton to Bournemouth

## SOUTHERN MAIN LINES
Basingstoke to Salisbury
Crawley to Littlehampton
Dartford to Sittingbourne
East Croydon to Three Bridges
Epsom to Horsham
Exeter to Barnstaple
Exeter to Tavistock
London Bridge to East Croydon
Orpington to Tonbridge
Tonbridge to Hastings
Salisbury to Yeovil
Sittingbourne to Ramsgate
Swanley to Ashford
Tavistock to Plymouth
Three Bridges to Brighton
Victoria to Bromley South
Victoria to East Croydon
Waterloo to Windsor
Waterloo to Woking
Woking to Portsmouth
Woking to Southampton
Yeovil to Exeter

## EASTERN MAIN LINES
Barking to Southend
Ely to Kings Lynn
Ely to Norwich
Fenchurch Street to Barking
Hitchin to Peterborough
Ilford to Shenfield
Ipswich to Saxmundham
Liverpool Street to Ilford
Saxmundham to Yarmouth
Tilbury Loop

## WESTERN MAIN LINES
Bristol to Taunton
Didcot to Banbury
Didcot to Swindon
Ealing to Slough
Exeter to Newton Abbot
Newton Abbot to Plymouth
Newbury to Westbury
Oxford to Moreton-in-Marsh
Paddington to Ealing
Paddington to Princes Risborough
Plymouth to St. Austell
Princes Risborough to Banbury
Reading to Didcot
Slough to Newbury
St. Austell to Penzance
Swindon to Bristol
Taunton to Exeter
Westbury to Taunton

## MIDLAND MAIN LINES
St. Albans to Bedford
Euston to Harrow & Wealdstone

Harrow to Watford
St. Pancras to St. Albans

## COUNTRY RAILWAY ROUTES
Abergavenny to Merthyr
Andover to Southampton
Bath to Evercreech Junction
Bath Green Park to Bristol
Bournemouth to Evercreech Junction
Brecon to Newport
Burnham to Evercreech Junction
Cheltenham to Andover
Croydon to East Grinstead
Didcot to Winchester
East Kent Light Railway
Frome to Bristol
Guildford to Redhill
Reading to Basingstoke
Reading to Guildford
Redhill to Ashford
Salisbury to Westbury
Stratford upon Avon to Cheltenham
Strood to Paddock Wood
Taunton to Barnstaple
Wenford Bridge to Fowey
Westbury to Bath
Woking to Alton
Yeovil to Dorchester

## GREAT RAILWAY ERAS
Ashford from Steam to Eurostar
Clapham Junction 50 years of change
Festiniog in the Fifties
Festiniog in the Sixties
Festiniog 50 years of enterprise
Isle of Wight Lines 50 years of change
Railways to Victory 1944-46
Return to Blaenau 1970-82
SECR Centenary album
Talyllyn 50 years of change
Wareham to Swanage 50 years of change
Yeovil 50 years of change

## LONDON SUBURBAN RAILWAYS
Caterham and Tattenham Corner
Charing Cross to Dartford
Clapham Jn. to Beckenham Jn.
Crystal Palace (HL) & Catford Loop
East London Line
Finsbury Park to Alexandra Palace
Holborn Viaduct to Lewisham
Kingston and Hounslow Loops
Lewisham to Dartford
Liverpool Street to Chingford
London Bridge to Addiscombe
Mitcham Junction Lines
North London Line
South London Line
West Croydon to Epsom
West London Line
Willesden Junction to Richmond
Wimbledon to Beckenham
Wimbledon to Epsom

## STEAMING THROUGH
Steaming through Cornwall
Steaming through the Isle of Wight
Steaming through Kent
Steaming through West Hants

## TRAMWAY CLASSICS
Aldgate & Stepney Tramways
Barnet & Finchley Tramways

Bath Tramways
Brighton's Tramways
Bristol's Tramways
Burton & Ashby Tramways
Camberwell & W.Norwood Tramways
Clapham & Streatham Tramways
Croydon's Tramways
Dover's Tramways
East Ham & West Ham Tramways
Edgware and Willesden Tramways
Eltham & Woolwich Tramways
Embankment & Waterloo Tramways
Exeter & Taunton Tramways
Fulwell - Home to Trams, Trolleys and Buses
Great Yarmouth Tramways
Greenwich & Dartford Tramways
Hammersmith & Hounslow Tramways
Hampstead & Highgate Tramways
Hastings Tramways
Holborn & Finsbury Tramways
Ilford & Barking Tramways
Kingston & Wimbledon Tramways
Lewisham & Catford Tramways
Liverpool Tramways 1. Eastern Routes
Liverpool Tramways 2. Southern Routes
Liverpool Tramways 3. Northern Routes
Maidstone & Chatham Tramways
Margate to Ramsgate
North Kent Tramways
Norwich Tramways
Reading Tramways
Seaton & Eastbourne Tramways
Shepherds Bush & Uxbridge Tramways
Southend-on-sea Tramways
South London Line Tramways 190?
Southwark & Deptford Tramways
Stamford Hill Tramways
Twickenham & Kingston Tramways
Victoria & Lambeth Tramways
Waltham Cross & Edmonton Tramways
Walthamstow & Leyton Tramways
Wandsworth & Battersea Tramways

## TROLLEYBUS CLASSICS
Bradford Trolleybuses
Croydon Trolleybuses
Derby Trolleybuses
Hastings Trolleybuses
Huddersfield Trolleybuses
Maidstone Trolleybuses
Portsmouth Trolleybuses
Reading Trolleybuses

## WATERWAY ALBUMS
Kent and East Sussex Waterways
London to Portsmouth Waterway
West Sussex Waterways

## MILITARY BOOKS
Battle over Portsmouth
Battle over Sussex 1940
Blitz over Sussex 1941-42
Bombers over Sussex 1943-45
Bognor at War
Military Defence of West Sussex
Military Signals from the South Coast
Secret Sussex Resistance
Surrey Home Guard

## OTHER RAILWAY BOOKS
Index to all Middleton Press stations
Industrial Railways of the South
South Eastern & Chatham Railway
London Chatham & Dover Railway
London Termini - Past and Present
War on the Line (SR 1939-45)